GW00870456

# Pablo Escobar

## -Sinner or Saint-

**Raymond Johnson**

Copyright 2016 by Raymond Johnson - All rights reserved.

This document is geared towards providing exact and reliable information in regards to the topic and issue covered. The publication is sold with the idea that the publisher is not required to render accounting, officially permitted, or otherwise, qualified services. If advice is necessary, legal or professional, a practiced individual in the profession should be ordered.

- From a Declaration of Principles which was accepted and approved equally by a Committee of the American Bar Association and a Committee of Publishers and Associations.

In no way is it legal to reproduce, duplicate, or transmit any part of this document in either electronic means or in printed format. Recording of this publication is strictly prohibited and any storage of this document is not allowed unless with written permission from the publisher. All rights reserved.

The information provided herein is stated to be truthful and consistent, in that any liability, in terms of inattention or otherwise, by any usage or abuse of any policies, processes, or directions contained within is the solitary and utter responsibility of the recipient reader. Under no circumstances will any legal responsibility or blame be held against the publisher for any reparation, damages, or monetary loss due to the information herein, either directly or indirectly.

Respective authors own all copyrights not held by the publisher.

The information herein is offered for informational purposes solely, and is universal as so. The presentation of the information is without contract or any type of guarantee assurance.

The trademarks that are used are without any consent, and the publication of the trademark is without permission or backing by the trademark owner. All trademarks and brands within this book are for clarifying purposes only and are the owned by the owners themselves, not affiliated with this document.

# Contents

# Introduction

We are all intrigued by the people who have or had a great influence on the society and world's history in any way. Those people often aren't simply good or bad; they are just humans, like all of us, with virtues and flaws. We can make decisions for ourselves if we agree on their work, ideas, and ways to accomplish those ideas they have. Judging often seems interesting, but is quite wrong on some levels, because we can never be sure what happened, why happened, and who really did what. Many events from the present time, or a few years old, can't be completely researched, and, let us don't forget: "history is written by the victors."

Popular media has a great influence on mass opinion, serving the selected data, and making its own interpretation of the lives and life events of people such as Pablo Escobar.

Pablo Emilio Escobar Gaviria (his full name) was born on December 1, 1949, in Antioquia, Colombia, and was well-known drug lord and a drug trafficker. He was also known by his incredible income, which most likely cannot be precisely estimated. He worked with other criminals who formed Medellin Cartel with him, and with such strong collaboration he managed to control over 80% of the cocaine shipped to US. It is said that at the pick of his carrier his wealth reached about $30 billion, even though there were many losses due to difficulty of money storage. There were times when they would just put money on a pile, so that the mice managed to eat it. Sometimes the money would be placed underground, in the holes, and the rain would ruin it. But, losses were still nothing compared to the profit.

While he used that wealth to support the poor, he also used it to gain full control over the government and politics in Colombia. He played different roles for different audience. While he used money and violence to gain control over the country leaders, judges and police, he used kindness and understanding for poor people, who saw saint in him. Having priests for friends, Escobar was quite saint-looking in the eyes of many. After all, who would expect from such calm man, walking next to those who are supposed to be modest and virtuous, to be what he really was, or what the part of him was?

Massive manipulation isn't so difficult to achieve, as we could see during the past few centuries, with some leaders who came out of nowhere and managed to gain incredible popularity over the average people. To get to understanding what kind of soil is just perfect for the rise of the unexpected heroes and villains, we need to learn a bit about the places where they have grown, taking a good look at the source of it all.

# Before Pablo

It wouldn't be a mistake to say that Colombia is a country with violence as a regular thing in its history. Just like any colonial country in the world, it had to be taken over by violence. When the Spanish conquistadors came, they had to face many native tribes, to conquer them. For some tribes, like Tairona, there was only one way – killing every last one of them. Considering all the evil newcomers have brought, makes you wonder if the centuries of violence are some sort of deserved justice.

During the 19th century there were eight civil wars between two great political parties. At the very end of the 19th century, in 1899, started the worst civil conflict of them all, called Thousand Days' War, which took over 100000 lives for the less of three years, destroyed economy and government. This made Colombian people scared and unable to truly trust one another. Besides that, it made them unable to trust their weak government who maintained power by using violence. They soon started to think about the robbers as the heroes of the nation. Robbers disobeyed the rules, disobeyed the law, and as such disobeyed the horrible government.

Most of the country territories belonged to a small group of rich, white Colombians, who used most of the natural resources to increase their wealth. The incredible difference in social status gave them the power to rule the land, controlling the government and limiting the chances for the poor to come out of their misery. Nobody cared about the education of the poor; no one cared if some of them died of hunger.

Poor people who worked for the rich, enjoyed the stories about robbers, who didn't only steal from the rich, but also managed to punish the rich, humiliate them, or even take their life. And, when it comes to taking of the life, they were quite creative. It would be wise to never search for what rituals some of the murderers had, because many of them are quite disturbing. We have probably all seen any horror movie in life, but real life terror is way more horrifying.

This wave of terror calmed down somewhere around 1953, when Gustavo Rojas Pinilla, an Army General, became the president of Colombia. Today, when the most of the world population prefers to embrace the democracy, we may think of it as a wrong choice. But, considering the mess Colombia was in, it's pretty understood able that that is the system they needed at the time. Unfortunately, this change came too late for the generations of children who were raised hearing stories about "heroes" of the people, learning about violence, and the stories in which the cruelest violence was justifiable.

Gustavo Rojas Pinilla was president for 5 years only, during which he enacted legislation that gave women equal rights to vote, constructed several hospitals, brought television to the country, constructed universities and National Astronomical Observatory. He conducted the great projects such as Atlantic railway, and hydroelectric dam of Lebrija, etc.

After his resignation the democratic system came to Colombia, or at least, some sort of democratic system. There were two political parties, Colombian Liberal Party and Colombian Conservative Party, and every 4 years there were elections, and change of leaders. Whatever reforms or social progress one government wanted to maintain, the next government would stop. This was anything but the system that worked.

# Early life

Escobar was born in Rionegro, in the Antioquia Department of Colombia. He grew up near Medellin, which will later become his real home. His parents were Abel de Jesus Dari Escobar, a farmer, and Hermilda Gaviria, an elementary school teacher. While they were hard-working people, who feared God and avoided all sorts of interfering with the criminals, the violence was all around them. Violent deaths were quite often, and they could only pray for the health and safety of all of their seven children.

Their children, like all others, were listening to the stories about famous robbers, and young Pablo loved them and admired them. Again, like many others. Back in those days, admiring the robber wasn't uncommon in Colombia. Considering that, it's not a great surprise that Pablo wanted to become one of them. After all, they were loved by many; they were feared, and respected. They had money and they were free. When we say "free," what we mean is free of all the rules society determined. There were situations when the famous robber was caught, but you will never hear about it in the folk stories. Even if their life ended with death, it was usually a heroic, brave death, something to be proud of. As many children today dream about having superpowers, like popular heroes, it is not surprising that Pablo wanted to be rich, famous and untouchable, which was the dream many children from poor families had back then.

For his parents, it was quite difficult to provide their children all they needed. There is a story, told by Pablo's son, which happened when Pablo was six years old. He started going to school, which was very far from his home, and every morning he had to wake up very early, because it took him very long to get there. But, he and his brother didn't mind that. They would go and walk, as long as it needed. The problem was that their shoes couldn't survive such road.

When his shoes got holes, he decided it's useless to wear them, so he came to school barefooted. What happened next is that the teacher didn't allow him to enter the school, but sent him home instead. After learning about what happened, his mother went to shop and stole a pair of shoes. Later on, when she confessed her crime to the priest, she brought them back, and took another pair on the credit.

From this experience Pablo sure has learned about how a moral person his mother was, but he also learned about humiliation, and how he won't avoid this horrible feeling unless he is rich and powerful.

The point of this story is not to sympathize with him, but to understand how it all started. This sense of social injustice made him think a lot, rather than playing with the other kids. He hated poverty, thinking how it literally invites misfortune.

When he got older, he joined street gangs, learning from them about cruelty, the trick, risks, and the common people. He started earning money hustling, he thought how he doesn't need school, so he stopped going there. Eventually, his mother managed to make him return to school, but it didn't take long before he was expelled due to his behavior on classes.

# Early criminal career

His criminal career started very early, but it's hard to determine how early exactly. There are stories about his involvement in the stealing of the gravestones, when he was a teenager, but his brother Roberto denied them. He said that the gravestones were removed by the graveyard keepers, if someone would stop paying the site care. Sebastian Marroquin, the son of Pablo Escobar, claims that the first steps his father took in the criminal activities were selling counterfeit high school diplomas.

Pablo Escobar was engaged in criminal activities such as selling fake lottery tickets, selling contraband cigarettes, and car stealing. When it comes to car stealing he was quite clever. Instead of stealing and trying to sell the entire car, he learned how to part out the car, so that he can only sell pieces, leaving no evidence of his crime. He gets very good in this: he could part out car in a few hours.

After he made a lot of money this way, he stopped parting out car, since it became easier for him to simply pay the corrupted cops and judges not to go after him. He managed to find the people who would sell him new, fake documents for the car he stole, for the right price. It made his job looking legal from on the surface. The next idea for the job that formed in Pablo's head was car racing. He had many cars and car parts in his storage, so designing the fastest car wasn't too difficult for him. The idea that followed was to sell protection, some sort of insurance back then. The cat owners would pay him to protect their car from stealing.

After stealing the cars he decided to steal people, or kidnapping. Pablo never did this on his own: he would always hire some local folks, and made sure that those folks can't be truly certain about his identity. At the beginning, he only kidnapped those who owe him money. Sometimes the family of the taken person had enough money to pay Pablo to let the person go. Sometimes they didn't, and the person was killed for it. Such murders were seen like a rational thing to do in order to protect Escobar's interests. Back in those days, the government wasn't able to protect anyone from the loss due to fraud, or inability to get money back from anyone who owes you. Pablo knew that when people see how dangerous and serious he is, they won't try to steal from him, to trick him, or to owe him.

But, there were times when he would kidnap and kill just to prove something. The most well-known case, even though it was never proven, was the kidnapping and killing of Diego Echavarria, a prominent businessman, in summer 1971. He was held hostage for over a month, and even though his family paid $50000 for his life, he was killed by el "Mono" Trejos, one of the Medellin gang leaders. It is still a mystery if his death was ordered by Escobar (who was called "el Doctor" after this murder), or was it the action of a few gang members who wanted to show how money can't save the rich from the bad things they're doing.

Diego Echavarria was respected in high circles, but he wasn't the boss anyone would like to have. He would often fire people from their work, and, as well as many other landlords, he would extend his territory by exiling people living in the villages near the river. Back in those days, many homes didn't have a sewerage system, so living near the water source was quite important. Landlords didn't care about this. In the end, it was not surprising that most of the people living in poverty praised Escobar for taking down one of those people.

# Rise of power

Since the old marihuana users started to discover cocaine, and use it more and more often, Pablo decided to start a new job. He realized that the US is his target market, and he found ways to ship great amounts of drugs (70 to 80 tons on a monthly basis). It didn't take long before the needs for cocaine became enormous. Escobar organized the transport of coca paste from Bolivia and Peru to America, usually to Florida and California.

He founded a Medellin Cartel, a powerful drug network, which had rivals in Colombia and abroad. This network was well organized, sending 15 tons of cocaine each day, which brought them $420 million on a weekly basis. With all this money, Escobar and his comrades started to live some of his wildest dreams. He purchased 7.7 square miles of land in Antioquia, on which he built Hacienda Napoles, a luxury house. The estate contained a zoo, a lake, a bullring, a sculpture garden. In 1987, his name appeared in Forbes magazine, since they noticed him as one of the richest men on the planet. He remained on the list for seven years in the row.

The money gained through the drug trafficking found its way all around Medellin. The money was coming fast, too fast and in such amounts, there was no enough time to invest it. New firms started to work, the unemployment rate drastically fell down, and new roads were built. Escobar personally had 19 homes in Medellin, and each of them had its own heliport. He had a fleet, of both ships and planes. With all this money, he was able to literally buy anyone and anything. As soon as he would hear about a new successful lab for cocaine production on his territory, he would take over it. Even if he would allow some small group the work on their own, they would have to pay him the taxes, for he provided them "a safe transportation." Almost like selling the "insurance policies" when he was younger.

Police investigators who tried to arrest him on a few occasions were found dead, many judges shared the same fate, if they wanted to work their job properly. There were those who would rather sell their dignity for a great amount of money, whether because they wanted to earn a lot, or because they simply preferred to stay alive. At the time, government and the judiciary of Colombia were still very weak, and judges were, like all other people quite unprotected. This system, in which people of the law could face bullets or receive money, was called by local people "plata o plomo."

Politicians in Medellin didn't really care about Escobar's actions, since they managed to earn pretty much thanks to him. In fact, the highest authorities, like President Alfonso Lopez Michelson and his administration, allowed the limitless conversion of US dollars to Colombian pesos and legal way to invest money in drug trafficking. The government was partner in crime, supporting it and pretending to be blind. Mostly because the president and everyone around him were supported by rich families, who also wanted to make money on the cocaine business.

Escobar was ready to make losses at some times, and to allow police to confiscate cocaine ready for transportation. The next day the media informed about the great action performed by the police, and the people believed that the authorities really do something against the drug trafficking.

The cartels had fought wars of their own, in order to become leaders in the job. Even when the hierarchy was finally established, there were wars whenever losses were made. These wars caused the deaths of many innocent people, whether due to poorly planned bomb attack, or due mistaking of someone's identity.

The strong wave of corruption flooded Colombia. Authorities in Bogota had no idea how much it's going to cost them.

# Role in politics

As he gained more and more power, Escobar started to think about his childhood dream: to become the president of Colombia. He knew that in order to achieve this, he needs to change his styling, and the image most of the people had about him. He started to claim how he never took part in illegal businesses, trying to show himself as a decent family man. He started to act politely, and he was especially interested in helping the poor.

He started to turn people against the authorities in Bogota, and against the US. It wasn't very difficult to achieve, on the contrary: most of educated youth supported the guerilla armies such as M-19, ELN and FARC, who fought against the private paramilitary unit, whose main task was to protect the rich families from the lynch. Escobar believed that in his own way, he successfully fought a war against US, since the cocaine he sent to the north did nothing but ruin the American youth, and the money that came from it, helped in rebuilding the country. In a way, he was Robin Hood, although he didn't actually steal from America, he was just selling the product someone wanted to buy. As he said in one of his interviews:"If cocaine was legal, they would call me businessman, and not a criminal."

He wanted to become a living legend, like Pancho Villa. He was obsessed with this Mexican, especially after he heard a story according to which Pancho was actually a Colombian. He liked to dress himself as Villa, imagining himself as the hero of the nation.

In 1978, he was elected for substitute city council member in Medellin. Besides that, he supported with money and resources both of the presidential candidates. In both cases, he stood beside the winner. Two years after, he supported the forming of the new political party – Colombian Liberal Party, whose leader on a local level (in Medellin) was ex Minister of Justice Alberto Santofimio, and the leader on the national level was Luis Carlos Galan.

In order to keep a good image in society, he paid journalists and publicists to write positive articles about him. He even founded his own newspapers, called "Medellin Civico", which represented him almost as a saint. Literally, there were articles regarding how some of his supporters see him, and some of them would say how "he has the hands of the priest," and "his eyes are filled with tears, because of the starving families."

During the 1979, Colombia signed an agreement with the US, and proclaimed that transportation of the illegal substances over the America's borders in crime against US. According to this agreement, Colombia had to extrude everyone who interferes with the drug trafficking business. Of course, since there were hundreds of people working in this industry, the attention was in the main bosses only. This made Pablo and others like him quite concerned. Since that moment he has used all of his power and popularity to ban the law.

In 1981, Pablo started to behave as many oligarchs in Colombia behaved before: as if he was above the common people and the law. He formed a private paramilitary unit, called "Muerte a Secuestadores" (meaning "Death to kidnappers"), to fight guerilla units that kidnapped rich people. It was quite absurd that Escobar, who was once well known by the kidnapping of wealthy people, formed an army to fight kidnapers.

Pablo started to make an influence on authorities to legalize drug trafficking. He knew that if he succeeds in this, the extradition law will be banned, and he won't have to lie about his job and the source of his wealth. His lies were quite creative. He used to say how he started a bicycle renting agency when he was 16. Then he said how he gained his money working with the prize games. At some moment he mentioned his car selling business, but he skipped how he used to steal cars, before the sale. All these made up stories were funny, especially considering that the entire Colombia knew the truth, and apparently, many people didn't mind this truth, as long as they could live their lives normally. Perhaps it was Escobar himself who wanted to believe that he was a successful businessman, rather than a criminal.

In 1982, Pablo became a congressman, which wasn't just great title for him, but was also a guarantee that no one will try to put his behind the bars. Colombian law provided immunity for diplomats. He also received the diplomatic passport, which allowed him to travel to America with his family. It's pretty ironic that he disliked America as much as he did, and yet decided to travel there with his family as soon as he could. He and his family visited Disneyland on this journey, as well as the White House.

During the 1983, when he tried to take his place in Congress again, he was denounced by Rodrigo Lara. Lara became the Minister of Justice after the leader of his party, Luis Galan, lost the elections. According to law, the new president had to give some ministry roles to his opponents. When Lara got his opportunity to search for dirty money, he didn't want to wait. He was brave, or silly enough to mention the investigation America started, in front of Escobar himself.

During a few months Lara worked to show Escobar for who he really was. Famous newspapers, such as El Espectador started publishing old case files, regarding the crimes Pablo were caught for in his early days. ABC-TV showed the documentary which marked Pablo as the greatest drug lord in Colombia. It didn't take long before Galan decided to expel Pablo from the party. Lara had a great support now, and was ready to agree on any extradition demanded by the US.

Escobar was under pressure and humiliated. Authorities have confiscated 85 exotic animals he held in Hacienda Napoles, because he brought them over the illegal channels. He claimed that his factories will stop their work, which will leave thousands of people jobless. He knew that his political career has already come to an end. And he blamed Lara for this. He couldn't understand that Lara simply wishes to clean the land of the illegal business; he believed that Lara works as someone else is telling him, someone from America, probably, or someone from Cali Cartel.

Lara was killed on April 30, 1984, with the seven bullets while driving, by the assassin on the motorbike. While he was concerned about the safety of his family, which he moved to Texas, he wasn't careful enough when it comes to his own safety. He wasn't even wearing his armor, although it probably wouldn't save him, anyway. The street in which the murder occurred now has the name "Avenida Rodrigo Lara Bonilla."

# Time in exile

Of all crimes Escobar has committed, not a single one has backfired on him like the assassination of Rodrigo Lara. Although Escobar personally funded the campaign of the president Belisario Betancur, the president turned against him, and all the other drug lords in the Colombia. Betancur gave orders to police to confiscate all the drug lords' properties. He also accepted the help of US in a war against major kingpins.

US were very interested in cooperation with the Colombian government, in order to defeat Pablo Escobar, who was blamed for the cocaine plague among the American youth. In June, 1986, Len Bias died after cocaine overdose. His death spread panic over the entire country. Suddenly, everyone started talking about the side effects of drugs and drug dependencies. While it used to be fun equipment for the parties, now it became a passive murderer.

Escobar tried to present the interfering of the US as the violation of Colombia's sovereignty. He claimed that it's nothing but outrageous to send away the sons of Colombia. Playing the patriotic card didn't work and he had to leave the country, until he is sure that he can safely return. He went to Panama, which he already earlier considered for a country with strategically good position for his job. But, this wasn't the place where he wanted to spend his life. It's pretty safe to say that Colombia had a special place in his heart, and during his staying in Panama, he worked on establishing a safe ground for him in Medellin.

He met with Alfonso Lopez, the ex president of Colombia, and Alberto Santofimio, the ex Minister of Justice. Escobar and Jorge Ochoa (one of the key members of Medellin Cartel) told them that they will stop with their work, and return all the money they keep abroad to Bogota, if the government can guarantee their safe return, leave them their homes, and guarantee that none of them will be extradited to US.

Although the proposal sounded nice, president Betancur had to reject it. Lara's assassination wasn't something easy to forget or forgive by the people. Even if Escobar was ready to stop with the drug trafficking business, most likely many other people working in the net (thousands of them) wouldn't agree with it.

He tried to work on new fields, but the paths he used now weren't as safe as those he had at home. He tried to work in Nicaragua, San Salvador and Panama, but in many occasions he escaped DEA (Drug Enforcement Administration) agents by pure luck. Due to his absence, he started losing control over the Medellin.

It was the kidnapping of his father that made him return to Columbia. Pablo didn't want to wait for deals and money transfer. Instead, he started a counterattack. Dozens of people in Medellin were killed, whether they had anything to do with the kidnappers or not. Pablo's father Abel had 73 years at the time, and he returned home safely. Those who kept him hostage were too frightened by Pablo's rage.

After this event, Escobar returned home, and he never left Colombia again.

# Los Extraditables

In 1985, Pablo again tried to make peace with the government, offering his surrender, as long as they can promise that he won't be extradited. After another rejection, he realized that he has to prepare for a long war.

In early 1980, he started gathering people like himself, criminals who wanted to avoid the possible cells and bars in the US, called Los Extraditables. They swore to fight extradition with all their might, even if it costs them their lives.

At the very beginning, all that this group did was publishing newspapers, which was quite a peaceful way to express their point of view, their goals, and reach the high authority as well as the common citizens. Pablo wrote many texts, and they were pretty successful at reaching the hearts of all true Latinos. Those texts were patriotic, claiming that although Colombia isn't strong enough to fight crime, it shouldn't allow other judges on their field. Again, he stood against the US, and warned that if the government won't stop agreeing to extradition, bloodshed will occur. As the government refused to show its weakness in front of the entire nation, the bloodshed did take place in the Palace of Justice itself.

On November 6, 1985, at 11:35 AM, 35 guerillas (from the groups called M-19) entered the Palace of Justice. Some of them entered through the basement, while others took the first floor and the main entrance dressed as civilians. Security guards were killed immediately, as well as the building manager. About 300 people were taken hostage, among which were 20 judges and 24 associate justices. Army troops reacted quickly, rescuing 200 hostages, during the next three hours since the attack started. Guerillas, who claimed that they have taken over building "in the name of peace and social justice," demanded from president Betancur to come to the Palace to face his justice. Of course, the president refused it.

The next day, in 8:30 AM, guerillas freed State Councilor Reynaldo Archiniegas, in order to allow the entrance of Red Cross, and initiate dialogue. But, the reaction of the army wasn't very peaceful. We can only assume that considering violent ways criminals in Colombia used during the previous years, the army had no option but to show violence themselves in order to show the Escobar and everyone else how furious government can be.

The army attacked with various weapons, among which were rockets that ironically, succeed in burning about 6000 criminal files, among which was the one of Pablo Escobar. At first it was believed that guerillas burnt these files themselves, but the ballistics experts suggested otherwise.

During these 2 days more than 100 people died. After this massive attack, complete justice system was paralyzed. Judges were scared for their lives, gathering the jury was impossible... The Supreme Court decided to forbid any extradition, due to fear.

This was a reason for great celebration among all those people working in the drug trafficking business, with Pablo on top. For this occasion he organized firework in Medellin. His newspapers informed about the great victory of Colombian people. Main editor of "El Espectador," Guillermo Cano, wrote about this in quite different way. He stated that Colombian people lost a battle against criminal, and that cartels took control over the entire Colombia. He was killed a few weeks later in his car.

# Assassination of Luis Galan

Although Escobar used to support the Liberal party, he lost his membership after the leader of the party, Luis Galan, decided to show his attitude toward the drug trafficking business. And, not just the business, but also the violence and corruption such business brought with it. He was extremely popular among the people of Colombia, and it was very easy to see that he will be elected for president on elections in 1990.

In his campaign he showed himself to be the enemy of the cartels, he was ready to clean Colombia of all drug dealers, and to send them away to US. This was what Escobar feared most. Galan had the support of the people, and Escobar knew that killing him would spread rage over the entire country. His feelings about this topic were surely mixed: he wanted to keep himself safe, but he also disliked Galan, maybe even hated him. Galan supported Lara, when Lara decided to follow the roots of "dirty money," when he spoke against Escobar in the Congress, destroying the possible path for Escobar to what he always wanted: to become the president of Colombia. Escobar had the power and money, so he obviously didn't want to become president for any of those things. He wanted to be loved. He wanted to be adored by the people. But, he wasn't loved; he was respected some time ago, while now he was just feared.

On August 18, 1989, Galan was killed as he walked onto the stage to give a speech in front of 10000 people in Soacha. More than 10 others were wounded during the attack.

Cesar Gaviria was proclaimed as Galan's successor. Since he decided to follow the path of Luis Galan, he became the new target for cartel attack.

On November 27, 1989, the bomb was placed in Avianca Airlines Flight 203, by the Escobar and Medellin cartel. Gaviria was supposed to be on that flight, but he wasn't, so the cartel didn't take the life of the person they wished, but they took 110 lives (107 on the flight, and three on the ground), among which were two American citizens.

By doing this horrible deed, Escobar brought his enemies closer together, and gave them more power and support then they had before. Gaviria became the president in 1990.

# Kidnappings, killings, and surrender

As Gaviria became president, Escobar decided to change his tactics in order to survive the war. Instead of bombing attacks, he decided to start taking hostages. Those hostages were members of most powerful and most influential families in Colombia. Escobar wanted to be considered for revolutionary, and not for criminal, and claimed that all he is doing is fighting a war against oligarchy, protecting the poor.

The first kidnapping occurred on August 30, 1990, when Diana Turbay, journalist and the daughter of former president of Colombia, was tricked into going to a supposed interview with a guerilla leader, Manuel Perez Martinez. Four members of her team were caught, too, but she was the main aim.

In October, Escobar lost his cousin in showdown with police. Three more criminals were extradited to US during the first few months of Gaviria's mandate. Gaviria wanted to make peace with cartels and especially with Escobar, before more people die or get hurt. In order to do so, he was ready to agree on prison sentence only for some smaller committed crimes. He also agreed not to send a single criminal to US. However, at this moment, Escobar wanted a lot more. Soon after, new two kidnaps happened. Francisco Santos, El Tiempo's editor, and Marina Montoya. Escobar demanded a special jail for himself and for the other criminals, and a protection for their families.

Escobar was careful when it comes to choosing the right victims. He knew how Colombia's elite cares about their safety, considering that they always considered themselves for untouchable. Family members tried to put a lot of pressure on Gaviria. They wanted to give Escobar and his comrades a whole different status, as if they are just a political party, rather than criminals. It would give them a full amnesty.

In the next period police tried to take down as many Escobar's comrades as possible. After the death of his cousin Luis, who was killed in police attack, he kidnapped Maruja Pachon. The entire nation wanted to make peace with Escobar, craving to end the violence. For the Christmas, Pablo preformed the act of good will, releasing three hostages, members of Diana's team. Within the next few months, three of his comrades decided to surrender to authorities, wanting to end their role in this war.

Escobar's life became a nightmare. Police were quick in discovering his hideouts; he was always on the run, unable to enjoy the comfort he get used to. His comrades were getting killed and ending in jail, his entire organization started to collapse. He wasn't able to control the drug trafficking business, so he started losing money. At the end of 1990, he realized that surrender is his only option, right after he arranges better conditions for himself.

The war between cartel and police continued, and after the new deaths of Escobar's comrades, he ordered the murders of two hostages: Marina Montoya and Diana Turbay. Gaviria had a massive burden on his heart, which totally crashed him after two more horrible deaths: the one of Low Murtra, former minister of Justice, and Fortunato Gaviria, president's close cousin who was buried alive. Gaviria was crushed, but still wasn't broken. Finally, Escobar started releasing the hostages, and surrendered.

## Staying in La Catedral

The prison in which Escobar served his sentence was anything but a place to suffer. His prison was a luxury home with bar, Jacuzzi, football pitch, gym, sauna, waterfall... His prison was a dream house for millions of other people. That was a place where he was supposed to find his inner peace, to stop all criminal activities, and that after some time get out as a free man and join his family. Since there were many corruptive judges in the past, he had a good reason to believe that sooner or later another one will show up, and let him walk freely outside. Truth is: he actually could walk outside. He often went to a nearby village to spend some time in clubs, in the company of numerous women.

But, restless as he was, he continued his work from the prison. He knew that telephone wasn't safe to talk, with police and American agents listening, so he trained pigeons for message delivery. He was surrounded with his comrades, and his lawyer visited him every week. As soon as his comrades brought something new to prison, they would bring the same thing for him.

To keep an eye on his family, he installed a massive telescope on his cell's balcony. From there he could watch his wife and kids wherever they were, even though they came often to visit him. He even celebrated his 42th birthday in prison, with family and friends, that's how much restrictive this prison was. For this birthday he received a Russian fur hat from his mother. They had a real feast, with stuffed turkey, caviar, salmon and many other meals made by his chefs.

People sent letters to him; some letters were love letters from women who adored him, some were letters from poor people asking him for money and help, and some were from people who simply respected him regardless of his actions. He often answered those letters, sending money for those who asked. Although he was in prison, he did have huge amounts of money nearby. He arranged with cousins and coworkers, to send him money in milk cans, which he would later hide in the holes he dug in the ground around the house.

Prison officers weren't able to control Pablo and his men. On the contrary, they used to bring water to the football field, when the prisoners stayed for too long playing the game, and they would even serve the beverages to prisoners, later in the evening. They were no threat to him, or his comrades. The real threat was outside, and the prison officers had to watch carefully if someone is about to attack. Escobar had many enemies, and all of them knew where he is. La Catedral was carefully designed for this possibility. It had hidden tunnels, in case of evacuation, it had enough of weapons hidden, and its geographical location was perfect. The estate was surrounded with fog during the entire night, so no surprise attack could be performed from the sky.

While he enjoyed his time in prison, his lawyers received new accusations. Escobar was accused of being directly responsible for Galan's assassination. On one of Pablo's estates police found evidences of his guilt in the assassination of Guillermo Cano.

Since the stories about the continuation of his work started to appear in the media, and after the discovery what kind of prison La Catedral actually is, authorities, US Embassy and journalists started to put pressure on Gaviria. Gaviria knew that La cathedral is nothing but a farce, but he still liked the peace Colombians had at the moment. He wanted to keep it that way as long as possible, but the US authorities weren't satisfied with that. The huge amounts of cocaine were delivered to America, and that's why Escobar and his drug trafficking business still were their concern.

The president had no option but to try moving Escobar to a different location, to a real prison. For this task, he sent army troops to La Catedral on July 22, 1992. But, careful as he was, Escobar realized what's going on before they managed to grab him. He escaped, and from that moment, to his last day he was on the run.

# Los Pepes

After the Escobar's escape, the new wave of bombing and killing hit Colombia. The worst was bombing attack in front of the bookshop in Bogota, in which 21 adults and children died, while over 70 were seriously injured. The very next day, La Cristalina, the hacienda of Pablo's mother Hermilda, was burned to the ground. Soon after this, the next attack on Pablo's closest family happened when two bombs exploded in front of Pablo's family houses. His mother and sister were injured in these attacks. Soon after, someone burned another of Pablo's houses. Police was confused, since they had no idea who organized these attacks. It led to conclusion that there is an illegal group working against the main drug trafficker. Agents of DEA agreed that these people did horrible things, but they saw them as "enemy of their enemy," so, not quite a friend, but a helpful hand working outside the law, where the legal groups couldn't step in.

It was guessed that Los Pepes was a group formed of either Escobar's enemies from other cartels, or group formed of people who lost their family member's due Escobar's attacks, or both. The group needed weapons, which required funds. It is most likely that their sponsors were families Moncada and Galeano, since Escobar openly marked them as his enemies. After Escobar's escape from La Catedral, these two families started recruiting mercenaries to fight Escobar. Each mercenary received about $29000 for joining this more or less famous group.

Some of the main supporters of the group were ladies. Dolly Moncada, the widow of William Moncada, was one of them. Right after the disappearance of William and others, Escobar sent message to Dolly, giving her two options: to give up all her estates, money and belongings, or to prepare for war. She decided to run away from home in Medellin, which was quickly searched for signs of where she might be. Three weeks after her escape, close associate of her husband, Norman Gonzales was kidnapped and tortured for 13 days. His kidnappers wanted to get information about Dolly's hiding place. Dolly didn't want to give herself to Escobar's mercy. She made a deal with the Colombian government. She gave up most of her belongings, and agreed to cooperate in finding Escobar. Instead, the government gave her protection.

Los Pepes swore that they will perform attacks every time Escobar commit an act of terrorism in which innocent lives are taken. After many months of Los Pepes counterattacks, some of Escobar's comrades decided to surrender in fear of their lives. Among those people were Pablo's brother Roberto and well known hit man Popeye.

On February the 3rd, 1993, the corpse of Luis Isaza was discovered. Around his neck was attached note with the message that was signed with "Los Pepes." Another 4 Escobar's people were found murdered that day. And, every next day new corpses appeared, about six of them each day. The number of Escobar's comrades was getting low, since some of them were murdered, some decided to surrender, and new ones weren't so interested to join the crew. Los Pepes worked for several weeks only, and yet they managed to scare Escobar like no one ever did. That's why Pablo tried to send his children to safe ground in America, but the children were stopped at the airport, before they managed to enter the plane. US Embassy gave statement for newspapers that the children will receive visas only if their parents show up in the Embassy.

Since he couldn't send his children away, he figured he needed to fight back. So, another bomb attack was performed under his surveillance. The result: 11 dead and over 200 injured. Los Pepes get even angrier, and decided to burn down two estates that belonged to Escobar's bankers. After this, Los Pepes started to attack Escobar's lawyers, too. On April 16, the corpses of Guido Parra and his 18 year old son were found. Apparently, 15 armed people kidnapped them, and killed them, leaving a message for Escobar. The message was signed with "Los Pepes," and stated that this murders were committed as a revenge for the latest bomb attack.

These latest murders made president Gaviria give statement in which he claims that Los Pepes are the group working outside the law, and that they can't be linked to police or the government. He even offered the $1.4 million reward for the information about this unit of death. Right after this statement, the group informed that they will stop with further actions, because they gave enough of support in the war against Escobar.

There were a few attacks performed by Los Pepes even after the statement they gave. The last one happened in summer 1993, on the estate of Roberto Escobar. Roberto's stallion Teremoto was castrated, and his trainer and jokey killed.

# Hunting Escobar

The main hunter of Pablo Escobar was general Martinez, who tried to retire after the first anniversary of Escobar's escape from the prison. He felt as if someone else might be more successful in completing this task, but also wished to return to his family. Due to the nature of his job, he had to be absent from family life, his children couldn't go to school regularly because of their safety...

His request was denied, so the only remaining option was to find and arrest Escobar. He continued with the search, and with the arrests of Escobar's mercenaries and comrades. In the beginning of summer 1993, the Medellin cartel was almost destroyed. Escobar's residencies were empty, robbed and burnt. Los Napoles was under the control of police. His cooperatives died, surrendered, or decided to work with police in exchange for protection. Still, the main boss was unreachable, moving quickly from one hideout to another. General gladly used the new technologies from America, such as portable locator devices. But, he had a problem requesting those. There weren't many officers who knew how to use those, and one of them was his own son. General wanted to keep his family away from the war, but he had to agree that his son's involvement might bring end to this chase.

It took several months before Hugo and his team proved that they are worthy. Portable devices weren't so advanced 20 years ago. Once they have detected the frequency on which Escobar and his son, Huan Pablo, communicate, their job was to decode what they were saying, since the other pair of father and son had a secret way of communication, in case of eavesdropping.

The plan for finding Escobar was based on one idea: to isolate him. Without support, friends, family, money, he should become an easy target. But, Pablo wasn't completely alone. His son, Huan Pablo, often spoke to him over the radio. He used to inform his father about the police stations, about the attacks on their family, about the conversations he had with the Medellin's district attorney.

In October 1993, Hugo's team located Escobar, in San Joze church in Medellin. All the location devices confirmed that he is talking to his son from the church, and since he had great supporters among the catholic priests, it wasn't surprising that some of them would try to help him in such dark times. But, the attack on the church was unsuccessful, because Escobar wasn't there. The police and CIA forces demolished the building, searching for the hidden rooms, hidden passages, anything, but they couldn't find him. Hugo was confused, and ashamed.

From that failed action, he decided to work separately, with two other cops and their portable locator device. During the period of separate search, Escobar continued to talk with his son, even 4 times per day. His son provided valuable information about the plans police might have. According to this information, Escobar could get the idea where are they going to strike next, so that he can move if necessary.

The police, Centra Spike and Colombian team for telemetric surveillance managed to detect Escobar's location. He was on the estate on the top of the hill, above the village Aguas Frias. Helicopters were above the estate, ready to get to the ground. Pablo used to talk to his son in 4 PM each day, so they waited for the conversation to start, hoping to catch him unprepared. The conversation started a bit late this time, at 4:07 AM. As he heard a Pablo's voice, the general ordered the attack. Over 700

36

policemen and soldiers with dogs surrounded the hill, searching for Escobar. But, he was already far away. Two women were found on the estate, and they confirmed that he was there, the very same day. After this, Pablo stopped communication with his son; aware of the danger he puts himself in.

But, there was the side effect of this major search for Escobar. While all the forces were focused on finding him, the other small criminals continued with the drug trafficking business. Since Hugo started to lose his will in these failed attempts to find Escobar, his father gave him an easier target: Juan Camilo Zapata. Martinez thought it's a good idea to give Hugo something to work on while they're waiting for Escobar to start calling his son again. On November 26, he managed to provide and lead a successful attack on Zapata. That's when everyone in police started to take his monitoring devices seriously.

# Death

The only thing that could be the cause of Pablo Escobar's wrong move was his family. When Maria and their children tried to enter Germany, they were arrested, and under a threat to fly back to Colombia, which was the worst place for them to be. They already received a lot of threatening messages, many of Escobar's comrades, cousins and cooperatives were killed, whether they committed a crime or not. It's not quite known how did Pablo manage to follow each step of his family members, but when he discovered what's going on, he tried to call president Gaviria. At first, everyone in Gaviria's office thought it was a joke, but soon they called the president, who refused to make a deal with Pablo. On November 30, he wrote a letter to the government, and sent it to newspapers to publish it, so that everyone can read it. He was full of anger, bitterness, and incredibly worried. At this time, it became more and more clear that he is no longer concerned about himself, how much he was about his family.

Pablo was very proud on his son in these hard times, and was sure that he will grow into a man strong enough to protect his mother and his sister. He gave him clever instructions, what to say, how to say, with whom to talk, what to remain silent. But, to be absolutely certain of their safety, he needed to send them away from his enemies. He talked to Huan about the foreign countries and their laws, giving him answers to questions they usually have when it comes to interviews for a visa. He hoped that they will manage to leave on time, so that he can either surrender, or continue his war. He felt as if the greatest injustice was thrown at him: when he was killing innocent people in his actions, he was considered for criminal, but when the army forces and Los Pepes killed innocent people in their actions, they were considered heroes.

Pablo called his family several times in hotel Tequendama, where the police held them. It gave Hugo a chance to track Escobar's location. And he was successfully located in his new home in Los Olivos. Instead of string attack with hundreds of cops and agents, police decided to slowly enter the nearby homes. They needed to act slowly and carefully, because they didn't know the exact Pablo's address. On the 1$^{st}$ of December, Pablo again talked to his family. It was his 44$^{th}$ birthday, so they all wished him all the best. During this conversation, Hugo tried to detect his exact location, but soon he realized that he was most likely talking from the car, which made him unable to track precisely.

On December 2, 1993, Pablo tried to call his family at 1 PM. Police was checking each call, so he had to lie about his identity. He said he was a news reporter, and even with this "cover" it took him a few attempts before they allowed him to speak to them. It was the last conversation they ever had. His wife, Maria, lost all hope. She was certain that someone will kill her and children very soon and almost accepted this fate. Pablo tried to bring her back to her senses, and then he talked to his son about the upcoming interview.

During this conversation, Hugo managed to locate Pablo's hideout. To be precise, he saw him through the window. Escobar made several mistakes at the same time: he spoke with his family for several minutes, giving Hugo more than enough time to track the call, and even when he realized that something was going on outside, instead of leaving the home or hiding, he decided to stand right in front of the window. If he hadn't done that, discovering the right entrance would rely on luck and nothing else.

Hugo informed his father about Pablo's location. General Martinez gave order his people to surround the house. Pablo's comrade, called Limon, tried to escape over the roof, but was taken down with a several bullets. Pablo saw what happened, and tried to stand against the wall, which offered some protection, and after a few seconds tried to run over the roof. Rain of bullets came from the street and from other nearby roofs. Three bullets ended his life, but the fatal was the one that entered his ear.

Aftermath of his death

When the time came for writing reports, there were disagreements. Some said that he came out unarmed; some said he had a gun, but didn't fire, and some said that he tried to shoot the policemen. This final scenario was told by Hugo Martinez himself, although it was quite surprising for Pablo to have such reaction. For all the months he spent running away from police, he learned that going against the army with a single gun is quite useless. Running away, or surrender (which he was prepared to do, anyway) would make more sense. The autopsy report provides basic facts: he was shot with three bullets, of which one hit his leg, and the one hit his torso. None of this would have him killed, but would hurt him enough so that he can't run away.

It was the third bullet that killed him, the one that entered his ear. It killed him instantly. Although there is a chance that all three bullets came from one of the snipers, it is most likely that two managed to take him down, while the third was shot from a short distance. Short distance means that either Pablo decided to end his life with his own hands, or that someone came to him after he was taken down with the first two bullets, and finished him.

Seven years later, this theory was confirmed. Pablo was indeed shot in the head from a close distance by one of the policemen, was the truth revealed by Colonel Oscar Naranjo. He knew what really happened, but knowing how all his men simply wanted to put this nightmare to an end, he didn't want to judge them. Apparently, arresting Escobar wasn't good enough. After all, he was caught once, and it only happened because he agreed to surrender. Even if we can find understanding for what they did, it is quite hard to accept the smiles they had on their faces in the photo they took above Escobar's corpse, such morbid and disturbing smiles. One more thing was disturbing: someone from Martinez's team decided to "play" with the corpse, by changing his description. The change was in mustaches: they were shaved to look like Hitler's.

While the government celebrated this murder, Pablo's family was in great sorrow. His widow was tired, but at peace. His daughter defended her father, saying how killing him was wrong. Of course, a nine year old girl probably knew almost nothing about his sins. His son, Huan, had to pull himself together. His first reaction was to swear on revenge, but he quickly came down to his senses, aware of the fact that more violence won't bring anything good for his family.

Besides his family, many Colombian people suffered, too. Thousands of people came to Pablo's funeral. They followed his coffin, tried to touch the coffin, or even his face. In this crowd, Pablo was celebrated. They believed (and, who knows, maybe they are right, at least a bit), that many crimes weren't even committed by Pablo, and that the violence he used was understood able, since he had to protect himself from the army and government.

Even today, his grave is surrounded with fresh flowers, and people from all around the world. Some come to see his grave as a tourist attraction, and others come to salute the figure they consider for heroic.

The death of Pablo Escobar didn't change a lot, when it comes to drug trafficking business. Since the main focus was on Pablo for many months, the other cartels, such as Cali Cartel, had a chance to bloom. Somewhere around 1995, most of them were captured or killed, too.

On October 28, 2006, Pablo's body was exhumed. Some of his relatives requested this, in order to take a DNA sample, to confirm the alleged paternity of an illegitimate child, and to stop the conspiracy theories which claimed that the person in the coffin isn't Escobar.

# Family life

Considering all his horrible deeds, it's hard to imagine Escobar as a father, or a husband. Especially, since he was quite interested in spending days and nights with young girls. But, he was very devoted to his family. When his father was kidnapped, he stormed at his enemies as if he was the devil himself. He didn't want to surrender to authorities unless they give his family a protection from his rivals.

His widow fled Colombia in 1995 with her children. She was aware of Pablo's way of life, and his infidelities, but was always there for him. She was used as a role model when it comes to other wives of drug traffickers. Members of the Cali Cartel, which was the greatest rival of the Medellin Cartel, gathered the recordings of her conversations with Pablo and replayed it to their wives to show them how they should behave toward their husbands. This was probably the main reason why the Cali Cartel didn't kill her and her children after Pablo's death, even though there were stories about possible revenge.

Maria and her children stayed in Mozambique, after which they moved to Brazil, and after they went to Argentina. She took a false name, and lived under it for quite a while before she revealed herself accidentally. After this, she was imprisoned for 18 months, which was the time investigators needed to realize that there is no way to link her recent business to any criminal or illegal activity. Now she lives under an alias in North Carolina. Asked what she liked about Pablo were several things: his smile, the way he looks at her, his desire to help others, and his compassion. She also said he was a great lover, and that he was always a gentleman around her.

Pablo showed a great care toward his daughter Manuela on many occasions. There were times when the entire family needed to stay in the hideout, and there was one of those times when Manuela became hypothermic. To keep her warm, Escobar decided to torch $2 million in crisp banknotes. Later, when he stayed in La Catedral, he brought a huge doll house for her to play when she comes to visit.

His son was one of the rare people who tried to talk with him about how wrong his actions were. He wrote the book named "Pablo Escobar, My Father," about the life with the great narco boss. He claimed that his father never allowed the business to step in between him and his family, that the family was his number one priority. He was only 7 years old when Pablo told him what he does for a living. It was right after the assassination of Rodrigo Lara. Although he was very young, the boy understood what mafia and criminals are; he saw them in the movies and pictured them as "bad boys."

However, he was glad that his father decided to be honest with him, rather than keeping him deaf and blind for real life happening around him. After this revelation, Pablo used to talk about his actions, as if he was confessing his sins to a priest. Juan heard about everything: kidnappings, murders, bombs... He would often argue with his father, because he always disapproved the violence. If he wasn't the son of narco boss, he would probably suffer for all the words he said, but his position gave him some power. He could never win this argues, because Pablo was full of justification for the crimes he had committed. But, it's quite certain that one of the main reasons Pablo decided to surrender and go to La Catedral, was "his pacifist son."

He says that his father's death was nothing but a suicide. After this event, remaining members of the family get closer together. Even today they all live very close to each other, and see each other every day. All of them still love Pablo, from whom they only received love and affection.

Escobar's sister, Luz Maria Escobar, tried to apologize to all the people who suffered due to her brother's actions. There were many family members who accepted her apologize, and even found a way to forgive her, her family, and above all else, her brother. For others, the wounds are still too deep to heal. She likes to remember him by his good deeds, as well as many other people who still come to visit his grave. She used to go to him with their mother, trying to convince him to stop all the bloodshed, but he always managed to convince them how the stories aren't true, he claimed that there were many lies in media reports.

On the 20th anniversary of his death, she organized a public memorial for all her brother's victims.

# Love and relationships

Escobar was 27 years old when he decided to get married. The woman, or a girl perhaps, he decided to marry was Maria Victoria Henao. She was only 15 when she married him, which required a special permission. Of course, with the right amount of money no permission was difficult to get. Maria's family discouraged this marriage, because they considered Pablo for socially inferior. That was quite strange reason for disapproval, considering the fact that Maria's older brother used to join Pablo in small-scale criminal activities. The pair had two children: daughter Manuela, and son Juan Pablo, who changed his name to Sebastian Marroquin, years after the death of his father.

Although he loved his wife in his own way, he obviously thought that life is too short to be committing to one woman only. Besides his one-night-girls, he had a few regular relationships.

Virginia Vallejo, Colombian author, journalist, and television anchorwoman, described her romantic relationship in her memoir "Loving Pablo, Hating Escobar" which was published in 2007. The relationship lasted for 4 years, from 1983 to 1987. She moved to America in 2006, when she decided to cooperate with the Department of Justice in high-profile cases. She was well informed about Escobar's and Medellin Cartel's activities, the political assassinations, and the war between cartels... She testified against Alberto Santofimio, a former Minister of Justice and an associate of Pablo Escobar, who was accused of conspiracy in the assassination of Luis Galan, a presidential candidate. According to her words, it was Santofimio who made pressure on Escobar to eliminate Galan before he becomes president and extradite him. She said that Santofimio is a real killer, even though he didn't pull the trigger himself. She also gave a detailed description about Escobar's role in the Palace of Justice siege. Escobar financed guerillas to perform the attack, but she claimed that a great mistake was committed by an army, which led to the massive killing of judges and M-19 members. Her accusations were confirmed by Colombia's Commission of Truth, which lead to a high-ranking former colonel and a former general been sentenced to 30 and 35 years in prison. When asked how she managed to fall in love with Pablo, knowing all the things he have done, she said that she fell in love with his good and generous side. While the other rich people in Colombia preferred to stay away from the poor, giving them nothing, Pablo loved to share his wealth with those in need.

Griselda Blanco, known as "Godmother of cocaine," never claimed to be romantically involved with Pablo, although there were rumors about their passionate relationship. She mentioned him in her diary quire often, but it's not a certain proof of the love relationship. They were rivals in the business, and both were very dangerous players, so perhaps there wasn't romance, but respect between these two.

# **Properties**

As he earned a lot of money, Pablo could afford himself to create or buy various residencies, houses, with one special place called Hacienda Napoles. Since he earned a lot of enemies, he really needed a lot of those houses, so that he can quickly and safely move across the Medellin when needed. Hacienda Napoles surely wasn't one of well hidden safe houses, since everyone knew where it is. It was Pablo's favorite place for parties, meetings, fun in general. The luxury estate contained colonial house, a sculpture park, a complete zoo with animals, which were brought there by helicopters. There were elephants, giraffes, hippopotamuses, exotic birds and many other animals. There was a plan to build a Greek-style citadel nearby, but the job was never finished.

Hacienda Napoles is turned into a safari-theme park, because of the zoo Pablo had on his estate. Bullfighting arena is turned into a museum of African culture. The zoo again has many animals. The place looks delightful, and is quite difficult to link it to happening that occurred a few decades ago.

Although he rarely went to America (he had a diplomatic passport for a short time), he owned an estate in the US under his name. His waterfront mansion in Miami Beach, Florida, was pink-colored, 6500 square foot luxury home, built in 1948 on Biscayne Bay. The mansion was seized by the government in the 1980s. In 2016, the demolition of the mansion started and many treasure hunters took the opportunity to discover the secrets this home is hiding.

What would be one of the wealthiest men on the planet if he didn't have a villa on the island? He would probably be afraid of water or incomplete, considering his need for, well, everything. His villa on Isla Grande is now half-demolished, ruined and overtaken by vegetation and wild animals. The estate had a large swimming pool, a helicopter landing pad, apartments, and a mansion.

# Charity work

What most of the people loved about Pablo was his generosity. Many ladies fell in love for him because of his affection toward those in need of his help. Growing in poverty himself, Pablo knew how the life is for most Colombian people. His childhood showed him how much the government and high-class people feel about the rest of the state: not at all.

That's why he wasn't like the rest of them when he became insanely rich. If someone needed a shelter, he would provide a residence. If someone needed a job, he would provide a work. People called him "Godfather," or "Robin Hood," because of all the support he provided to society. He constructed numerous shelters, paved the roads, funded soccer teams, and constructed football fields (football was one of his favorite sports), he built many churches, hospitals and schools all over the country. He openly supported education, even though he himself never finished it, since he joined street gangs too early. Perhaps at some point he realized that the life of the criminal isn't the life he wanted for his children.

Whenever there were cultural events in the city, whether a concert or the opening of the art gallery, he would come there, sometimes as an honorable guest, and sometimes as a silent observer, and every time he would support the event with his money.

We can all agree that his money was "dirty," but it's still a lot better that he had an urge to share it with others. Without his work and his generosity, who knows how long would it take for Colombia to prosper? After all, many people who never interfered with crime claimed that their lives became horrible again after Escobar's death. With him gone, there was no one to help them.

# Conclusion

What can we come with, summing all we learned about a life of one extraordinary man? Can we salute him, or curse? It depends on the point of view. Many people in Colombia still cry over the graves of those who died in bomb attacks organized by Escobar, while many others still live in poverty with no one to turn to, no one to provide them support, or at least to honestly care about them.

We can never be certain how Pablo felt toward his people: did he play the role, or did he actually care? Even when he was on the run, in his hideouts, and when his resources were getting dry, he never refused to help those who asked for his help. Of course, there is a chance that he expected help later in return, but we could never know that. After all, how many good deeds are completely selfless?

Again, if he cared so much, why didn't he surrender a long time ago? Wouldn't it prevent the deaths of many innocent people as well as his? Remember what we told you in the beginning of the book. Colombian people adored criminals for generations, seeing them as the last resort against greedy landlords and government that never provided help or support. Morality and justice aren't something we can measure; it doesn't have the color, shape or size. It's something we feel as right, what we believe in. In the country where the law system was incredibly corrupted, like it was in Colombia, justice wasn't something you could achieve on the court.

Therefore, let's just try not to judge him, or anyone who behaved in the way we would never consider for moral or normal. Let's just agree on the great role Pablo Escobar had in the creation of modern Colombia, the country built on blood, the country whose history carries the burden of horrible violence. Let's try to understand and forgive everything that has been done. Who knows what we would do, if we were born then and there?

Hope is the only thing that remains, always. And, when it comes to this story, we can only hope that everyone affected by the life and death of Pablo Escobar have found peace. Let's hope he is at peace, too.

25054761R00031

Printed in Great Britain
by Amazon